MW00567270

A   Baby   Memory   Book

Welcome Home

Little One

Ellyn Sanna

A DayMaker Greeting Book

Where did

you come from,

baby dear?

Out of the everywhere into here.

O young thing,
your mother's lovely armful!
How sweet the fragrance
of your body!

—EURIPIDES

Welcome!

A woman giving birth to a child has pain because
her time has come; but when her baby is born
she forgets the anguish because of her joy
that a child is born into the world.

JOHN 16:21 NIV

Baby's Name: **Maya Lydia Noelle Mckie**

Born to: **Anthea Mckie**

Born on: **July 28th** at **3.21** am/pm

Weight: **6** lbs. **15** ozs.

Height: **54** cm/inches

Color of Hair: **Black**

Color of Eyes: **Black**

Mother's Thoughts: **I felt B truly Blessed to have you in my life. You came into the world surrounded by lots of love. Grandma cut your umbilical cord. Auntie Nelly was taping. Daddy was crying tears of Joy.** ♡

IF YOU'RE A NEW PARENT, BE PREPARED...

- ♥ to feel like you're in love.
- ♥ to spend most of your baby's first month just looking at him or her.
- ♥ to think everything about your baby is lovely and amazing: her tiny hands and feet; the way she yawns; the shape of her mouth when she's sleeping; the small, contented noises she makes when she eats.
- ♥ to cry the first time he gets his shots.
- ♥ for total strangers to touch and talk to your baby—and for them to always get her sex wrong.

Your baby's first cry is the one you hear in the delivery room, the triumphant, tension-shattering sound that says, "I'm here, I'm breathing, I'm alive!"
—KATHERINE KARLSRUD

Childbirth ends our pregnancies,

just as death will one day end this life's limitations.

When that day comes, when we are born from death's

darkness into a brilliance brighter than any we've ever seen,

will we experience the same sense of wonder

and recognition we feel at our baby's birth?

—ELLYN SANNA, *MOTHERHOOD: A SPIRITUAL JOURNEY*

Now we see but a poor reflection; as in a mirror;

then we shall see face to face. Now I know in part;

then I shall know fully, even as I am fully known.

—1 CORINTHIANS 13:12 NIV

To see what you have made coming forth from within you,

and in that moment of first vision, to love it totally and

for always. . . . Can anyone who has not given birth, in fact

or in imagination, understand what it means

for God to have created us?

And will the sight of God in heaven be like this, when after

unbearable pain and waiting the hidden is made known?

—MARGARET HEBBLETHWAITE, *MOTHERHOOD AND GOD*

Dear Lord,

Thank You for giving me this amazing miracle—
my baby. Just looking at her fills me with wonder
and praise. Thank You for each tiny part of her,
each fingernail and hair, each brain cell and blood
vessel. I am filled with awe and love for her—
and for You.

You knit me together in my mother's womb. . . .
I am fearfully and wonderfully made. . . .
My frame was not hidden from you when I was made in the
secret place. When I was woven together in the depths of the
earth, your eyes saw my unformed body.
—PSALM 139:13–16 NIV

An Awesome Responsibility

I am holding you by your right hand—
I, the Lord your God—and I say to you, Don't be afraid;
I am here to help you.

ISAIAH 41:13 TLB

Who visited your baby in the hospital?

During the 1½ days I was in hospital
the entire family came to visit you.
We had min 8-10 ppl in the RM. true Mckie style.
Auntie Gracelyn gave you your first bath :)

What gifts did they bring?

We had a baby shower 1mth earlier
so we didn't get gifts at the hospital
but everyone bought use food so
mommy & Daddy could eat. :)
. Grandma & Auntie bought me a
MK Diaper bag ♡

What did your baby wear home from the hospital?

I had this cute outfit picked
out for you, but you where
way too small for it. You ended
up wearing a winnie the pooh onesies.

Mother's Thoughts: _____

We were all so excited
to take you home. Grandma
drove us home, it took awhile
because she did not drive on highwa
we also had to stop off at fire station

I remember leaving the hospital. . .thinking, so they coul
"Wait, are they going to let me just walk off with him? but car
in proper
. . .I don't have a license to do this.

[We're] just amateurs."

—ANNE TYLER

Except that right side up is best,
there is not much to learn
about holding a baby.
There are one hundred and fifty-two
distinctly different ways—
and all are right!
At least all will do.

—HEYWOOD BROUN

It is still the biggest gamble in the world. . . .
It's huge and scary—it's an act of infinite optimism.

—GILDA RADNER

WHEN YOU'RE A NEW PARENT, BE PREPARED...

- to find that taking care of your baby is the hardest job you've ever had.
- to wish you could hurt in your baby's place.
- to wonder why you ever thought that the work for which you get paid was a hard job.
- to envy parents who make it look so easy.
- to feel more frustrated, more discouraged, and more incredibly joyful than you've ever felt before.

My only advice is to stay aware, listen carefully,
and yell for help if you need it.

—JUDY BLUME

New parents quickly learn that raising children
is a kind of desperate improvisation.
—BILL COSBY, *FATHERHOOD*

Parenting a little one at best is overwhelming—
overwhelming in the emotion, time, energy, and
decision making it takes. Did you ever imagine that
one so tiny, so longed for and sought after, could
be so intrusive of every area of your life? Day or
night, with no regard for people, venue, or time;
feeding, diapering, and consoling must take place.
. . . If you are tempted to be overwhelmed today with
feelings of inadequacy, step back and remember that
in spite of others' condemnation and misperception,
Jesus affirmed Mary. "She has done a beautiful
thing to me. . . . She did what she could."
—RUTH TUTTLE CONARD, *DEVOTIONS FOR NEW MOMS*

Children are like wet cement. Whatever falls
on them makes an impression.
—HAIM GINOTT

Today, God,

You know I didn't feel up to this enormous job You've given me. The baby never stopped crying, it seemed, not since five o'clock this morning. I'm so tired. There's so much I should be doing, so much for which I'm responsible. I don't know how to do it all. I feel overwhelmed.

Thank You, God, for being with me. I hear Your quiet voice reminding me, "I love you, child. Remember—you are not the source of your baby's salvation. I am. Put your baby in My hands and rest now. I alone can love him perfectly—just as I love you. I will help you carry this awesome responsibility joyfully."

What a relief, dear Father, to lean on You. And what comfort to know Your angels are helping me take care of my baby.

I tell you that their angels in heaven always
see the face of my Father in heaven.
—MATTHEW 18:10 NIV

Lullaby

Hush, my dear,

lie still and slumber,

Holy angels guard thy bed!

Heavenly blessings

without number

Gently falling on thy head.

—Isaac Watts

Smiles and Laughter

We were filled with laughter, and we sang for joy....
Yes, the Lord has done amazing things for us! What joy!

PSALM 126:2-3 NLT

Your baby's first smile:
Date __At Oct 26th/13__ Age __11 wks 5days__

Who your baby smiled at: __Mommy of course :)__

Your baby's first laugh: __Not sure the Date__

Date _____ Age __8-9 wks old__

What made your baby laugh: __You always laughed in your sleep.__

Mother's Thoughts: _____

__I wish I knew what you were__

__laughing about. :)__

_____

IF YOU'RE A NEW PARENT, BE PREPARED...

- to find yourself falling in love all over again
  the first time your baby smiles at you.
- to discover that blowing on your baby's tummy
  is the funniest thing you ever did.
- to wake up one morning and hear your baby
  laughing out loud, all by herself in her crib.
- to find yourself doing anything at all, no matter
  how silly or undignified, just to hear your baby
  laugh.
- to think that playing peek-a-boo is the high point
  of your day.

When we hear a baby laugh, it is the loveliest
thing that can happen to us.
—SIGMUND FREUD

When the first baby laughed for the first time,
the laugh broke into a thousand pieces and they all went
skipping about, and that was the beginning of fairies.
—J. M. BARRIE, PETER PAN

Babies smile from the moment they're born—but you're
never really certain they're smiling at you. "Gas
bubbles," your mother and mother-in-law will tell
you (although why a gas bubble should produce a smile
in an infant when it doesn't later in life, I've never
known). At any rate, those early smiles are fleeting,
and they seem distracted, as though the baby's
thoughts were turned inward to some weighty matter.

But then one day, when your baby's a month or
two old, she meets your eyes and gives a wide, gummy
smile of pure joy. You're startled, amazed, awed,

delighted; you realize for the first time the miracle of a simple smile. A mere stretching of our facial muscles communicates so much to each other, more than any word, more than any book.

Up until now, your baby's been a solemn little person. You love her more than you thought possible, and she's so close to you that she's almost inside your skin. But when she studied your face with her bright intent eyes, you were never quite sure what she was thinking. All these weeks you've been stumbling around in exhaustion, caring for this infinitely beloved little person who could express her appreciation only by ceasing to cry—but now she's rewarded you with this amazing smile.

She looks as surprised and delighted as you feel, as though she suddenly got the punch line of a joke she's been hearing for weeks. Her smile pulls you close to her in a way you haven't yet experienced. You find yourself totally engaged with her personhood, the unique individual she is.

What is overpowering is simply the fact that a baby is life.
It is also a mess, but such an appealing one that we look
past the mess to the jewel underneath.
—BILL COSBY, *FATHERHOOD*

Dear Lord,

Thank You so much for my baby's smiles. Her

laughter fills me with joy. She is so precious to

me, God. I don't have enough words to express

my love and gratitude. All I can say is thank You.

Lullaby

You are my sunshine,
my little sunshine.
You make me happy
when skies are gray.
You'll never know, dear,
how much I love you.
Please don't take my sunshine away.

Sleepless Nights,

Exhausting Days

"My grace is sufficient for you, for my power is
made perfect in weakness."
2 CORINTHIANS 12:9 NIV

First time your baby slept through the night:

Date Oct 25th Age 11 wks

Mother's Thoughts: You went to sleep at
0100 AM & did not wake up until
0800. I was happy for you, unfortunately
I was awake watching you sleep.

WHEN YOU'RE A NEW PARENT, BE PREPARED...

- to do anything to get your baby to sleep,
  including driving around the block twenty times
  at eleven o'clock at night.
- to wake up terrified that he's dead the first time
  your baby sleeps through the night.
- to find that greeting card and laundry soap
  commercials bring tears to your eyes.
- to wish that parenthood came with lunch breaks,
  vacation days, and sick time.
- to have the phone ring as soon as your baby
  falls asleep, startling him into a crying spell.
- to smell like sour milk a lot of the time.
- to find that your baby needs his diaper changed just as
  company walks through the door.

Having a family is like having a bowling alley installed in your brain.
— MARTIN MULL

I actually remember feeling delight, at two o'clock in the morning, when the baby woke for his feed, because I so longed to have another look at him.
—MARGARET DRABBLE

With our first child, that first night home from the hospital was a living nightmare for me. If she snuffled, I flew to the bassinet. If she was quiet, I also flew to her side, certain that I had somehow smothered her. Oh, that I had listened to a loving husband's advice (I wrongly thought him quite callous at the time!) and remembered that we had done our best, I needed to sleep, and God was awake, watching over us all!. . . And He never goes to sleep. When you are bending over this soft little bundle in the night to lift her, comfort her, diaper her, or feed her, remember that your heavenly Father is bending over you.
—RUTH TUTTLE CONARD, *DEVOTIONS FOR NEW MOMS*

I lift up my eyes to the hills—
where does my help come from?
My help comes from the Lord,
the Maker of heaven and earth.
He will not let your foot slip—
he who watches over you will not slumber.
—Psalm 121:1–3 NIV

There never was a child so lovely
but his mother was glad to get him asleep.
—Ralph Waldo Emerson

Babies are always more trouble than you thought—
and more wonderful.
—Charles Osgood

Dear God, You know how much I love my baby. I'm so glad You gave him to us; I love him so much. Help me remember, Father, that one day he'll sleep through the night—and so will I again. One day I won't have to change his clothes five times a day—or mine either. One day again I'll have time to do work I enjoy, talk on the phone with a friend, read a book, or clean my house.

In the meantime, God, help me to keep my eyes fixed on You. Remind me to rely only on You for strength. I know You will see me through this joyful, exhausting time.

All your doctor visits I got help by Grandma, Auntie priso & Dad. :)

. Before you were born Auntie Nelly & Auntie Andrea were the only 2 ppl that knew you were going to be a Girl.

Marriage and Babies

". . .the two are united into one."

Each man must love his wife as he loves himself,

and the wife must respect her husband.

EPHESIANS 5:31, 33 NLT

Your baby's weight at:

One month: 7 lbs 2 oz

Two months: 7 lbs 14 oz

Six months: 15 lbs 7 oz

Nine months: 18 lbs

One year: 21 lbs.

Mother's Thoughts: The 1st month we had to visit the doctor g wk. to check your wgt because you lost more then the 10% allowed after Dc from hospital I had to breastfeed you g 2hrs. in order to fatten you up. Your auntie also wanted you to be a fat baby. I use to call you my skinny dumpling. At birth you g wgt 2lbs 10oz

When you have a baby, you set off an explosion in your marriage,
and when the dust settles, your marriage is different from
what it was. Not better, necessarily;
not worse, necessarily; but different.

—NORA EPHRON

WHEN YOU'RE A NEW PARENT, BE PREPARED...

- to be too exhausted for romantic moments.
- to have the baby start to cry if you ever do feel romantic.
- to find that your baby's gastrointestinal habits have become your favorite topic of conversation.
- for seeing one movie a year in the theater—and falling asleep when you try to watch one together on the VCR.
- to call home eight times the first time you leave the baby with a baby-sitter.
- for the fact that weekends and vacations together will never be quite the same.

IF YOU'RE A NEW MOTHER, BE PREPARED...

- to be the one who always wakes up when the baby cries.
- to have it take longer to wake your husband up than it would to just get up and take care of the baby yourself.
- to feel a little jealous if your husband gets to escape and go off to work and you don't.

IF YOU'RE A NEW FATHER, BE PREPARED...

- to think your baby sleeps through the night six months before she really does.
- to have your wife hand you the baby with a desperate look on her face as soon as you walk through the door at the end of the day.
- to feel a little jealous if your wife gets to spend more time with the baby than you do.

Having a child is surely the most beautifully irrational act
that two people in love can commit.
—BILL COSBY, *FATHERHOOD*

Having a baby changes your marriage forever. For at least the next eighteen or so years, the two of you will be less spontaneous, less focused on each other. The time you have for each other will be more limited, and you will be more emotionally drained when you are together, more apt to vent your frustrations on the other. But even though that's true, the fact is, this baby ties you even tighter to one another than before. No one else loves him quite as much; no one else thinks he's quite as fascinating and handsome and intelligent. This baby pulls the two of you together in a knot that can never be broken.

I begin to love this little creature, and to anticipate his birth
as a fresh twist to a knot, which I do not wish to untie.
—MARY WOLLSTONECRAFT

God, our baby has enriched our marriage so much—and yet she also drains our marriage, puts a strain on it that wasn't there before. Sometimes being a parent is such hard work—and being married is hard work too.

And yet in the midst of all this hard work, You give us such joy. Keep our commitment to each other strong and firm, even when we're tired and cross. Help us to support one another and forgive one another.

Thank You for our marriage, Father. May it be a strong shelter for our child, a place where Your love and joy can dwell.

Lullaby

Hush, little baby,
don't you cry,
Daddy loves you
and so do I.

Messages from God

Long to grow up into the fullness of your salvation;

cry for this as a baby cries for his milk.

1 PETER 2:3 TLB

Milestones

Baby's age when he or she...

Rolled over for the first time: 4mths old Dec/13- Aunty Kelly Taped it!

Ate first solid foods: 6 mth- Jan 28th- Rice Cereal

Sat up alone the first time: 5mths old 2wks = Jan 2014

Crawled for the first time: 5mths 3wks Jan 2014

Stood up: 12mth

Took a first step: 12-13mths

Mother's Thoughts: Was so happy enjoyed taking you to the mommy & me classes to do singing + playing with others parents & kids.

Think always that, having the child at your breast,
and having it in your arms, you have God's blessing there.
— ELIZABETH CLINTON

WHEN YOU'RE A NEW PARENT, BE PREPARED...

- to sense God's quiet presence while you rock
  your baby to sleep.
- to understand in a new way what it cost God
  to send His Son to earth.
- to catch sight of God's face in the unconditional
  love your child gives you.

Every child comes with the message
that God is not yet discouraged of man.
— RABINDRANATH TAGORE

"I stinky," my toddler says and holds up her arms to me, smiling confidently. I put off the moment as long as I can, I must admit, but eventually I scoop her up and lay her on the changing table.

As I clean her, she chatters to me about Pooh Bear and Grandma and Daddy-at-work. I shake powder, then bend and blow on her tummy. She wiggles with delight, beaming up at me. Face-to-face, we smile at each other, exchange kisses, and I realize that her dirtiness was actually an opportunity for communion between us. . . . We are to have this same attitude of confidence and love toward God. . . the same delight in His presence that our children have in ours. Even our mistakes, our selfishness and failure, can be opportunities for communion with God. . . . Our recognition of our need for God's cleansing should be as simple, as automatic, as confident as my daughter's "I stinky."

. . .God's grace is not the stern thing we always thought. Instead, it is simple and joyful as a child's love for a mother or as a mother's love for a child. We do not have to strive and labor to merit this love; it simply pours down on us, moment by moment, no matter what we're doing. It frees us from the need to achieve, to prove ourselves. Like a child rocked in a mother's arms, even asleep we are nestled in grace.

—ELLEN SANNA, *MOTHERHOOD: A SPIRITUAL JOURNEY*

It is not a slight thing when they,
who are fresh from God, love us.
—CHARLES DICKENS

Dear Jesus,

Thank You for showing me Your love through my baby. When I watch him sleeping in his crib, when I listen to his soft coos and crows of laughter, when I feel his small arms around my neck, I sense Your presence with me. Thank You for this little love letter from You to me. Accept the love and care I give to him as a love gift back to You.

As a mother comforts her child,
so will I comfort you.

ISAIAH 66:13 NIV

Lullaby

Rock-a-bye baby,
thy cradle is green,
Father's a nobleman,
Mother's a queen.
Sister's a lady
and wears a gold ring,
And Brother's a drummer,
drums for the king.

Always your Baby —

and Always God's

"I am the woman who stood here that time praying to the Lord!
I asked him to give me this child, and he has given me my request;
and now I am giving him to the Lord for as long as he lives."
So she left [the child] there. . .for the Lord to use.

1 SAMUEL 1:26–28 TLB

More Milestones

Your baby's first words: DaDa

Your baby's first-birthday guests: Grandma, Auntie Jhanelle Krissy, Auntie Cindy, ~~Earl~~, Kyle, Lyli, Andrew, tanisha Randy.

Your baby's first-birthday presents: Grandma- clothes/toy Aunty Cindy + family = books + clothes

What your baby did: Smiled + grabbed cake c your hands.

Mother's Thoughts: " Was so happy that you were 1yrs old. Sad that I dropped your cake in the car!! But I dont think you cared or noticed... lol.

Your children are always your "babies,"
even if they have gray hair.
—JANET LEIGH

WHEN YOU'RE A NEW PARENT, BE PREPARED...

- to have your heart ache every time you and your baby
  are separated.
- to be a little sad as you watch your baby change
  so fast.
- to feel your heart go out to every parent whose
  child is in trouble.
- to lie awake worrying more than you ever did before.
- to wish you could somehow guarantee your child a
  perfect world.
- to find that the only answer to your fears lies in God.

Suddenly I realize that the sheer intensity of my love cannot protect this child from the perils of life. Spinal meningitis. Playground tragedies. Traffic accidents. God, I cannot stand it. My chest contracts with unborn grief. My breath comes quickly. To risk love is to risk loss. Shadows stretch across the living room and across my mind. And then I hear it. The still, small voice saying gently, deep inside, "You're not a proud new owner. You're a trusted caretaker. This is My child, and I've lent him to you. Love him dearly, but hold him freely. Trust Me for the days ahead."

—SANDRA BERNLEHR CLARK, IN A MOTHER'S TOUCH

Children are the living messages we send to
a time we will not see.
—JOHN W. WHITEHEAD

Dear God,

Help me to put my baby in Your hands each day of her life. You are her only safety, Lord. I know You love her even more than I do, and I trust You to care for her all the days of her life, no matter what. When worries attack me, remind me to give each fear to You. Thank You for the peace You give my heart.

We can't give our children the future,
strive though we may to make it secure.
But we can give them the present.
—KATHLEEN NORRIS

"Before I formed you in the womb I knew you,
before you were born I set you apart."
—JEREMIAH 1:5 NIV

Sleep, baby, sleep,

Thy father guards
the sheep.
Thy mother shakes
the dreamland tree,
And down drops pretty dreams
for thee.
Sleep, baby, sleep.

© 2003 by Barbour Publishing, In

ISBN 1-58660-820

Cover image © P. E. Reed/Photon
Book design by Kevin Keller | designconcep

Published by Barbour Publishing, In
P.O. Box 719, Uhrichsville, Ohio 44683, www.barbourbooks.cu

Member of the
Evangelical Christian
Publishers Associati

Printed in Chir
5 4 3 2